MW00772117

How To Overcome Anger, Bitterness & Unforgiveness

How To Overcome Anger, Bitterness & Unforgiveness

Reverend
Paul A. Tribus

WinePress Publishing
MUKILTEO, WA 98275

How to Overcome Anger, Bitterness and Unforgiveness
Copyright © 1997 by Paul Tribus

Published by:
WinePress Publishing
PO Box 1406
Mukilteo, WA 98275

Cover by **DENHAM**DESIGN, Everett, WA

All rights reserved. No part of this publication may be reproduced, stored in a retrieval system or transmitted in any way by any means, electronic, mechanical, photocopy, recording or otherwise, without the prior permission of the publisher, except as provided by USA copyright law.

Printed in the United States of America

Library of Congress Catalog Card Number: 96-61942
ISBN 1-883893-87-9

REVIEWS

"As a personal and close friend of Pastor Tribus for over 20 years, I am pleased that God has opened his heart to reveal to us some of the personal struggles and healing which God has brought him through. Like rays of sunshine and wells of refreshing the chapters of this book will serve as key to unlock doors to emotional healing for many who have been scarred by life's battles."

Rev. Gerald Davis, Senior Pastor, Rock Church, Petersburg, Virginia

"I really appreciated the Biblical way you treated the subjects of anger, bitterness, and unforgiveness. Your references to your own struggles and victories was outstanding. The honesty in which you revealed the problems personally, and the skillful way you presented it, and the ultimate victory is powerful!"

Rev. Leonard Fox, Founding Pastor, Inland Christian Center Church, Colton, California

"Paul Tribus has placed his finger on the pulse of anger, revealed its roots and has given the Christian a Biblical Solution. Paul, I enjoyed it thoroughly, Congratulations!"

Rev. Richard Hilton, Senior Pastor, Calvary Church, Johnson City, Tennessee

"A much-needed book written from Paul Tribus' life experiences. You can find joyful spiritual victory in these pages. The list of 'stress relievers' is worth the read."

Del Wantland, National Director, Point Man International Ministries, Sheridan, Michigan

"The Bible gives us an example of a man by the name of Paul the Apostle. He learned a life of control in that he knew how to be abased and how to abound, everywhere and in all things, and to be full and hungry. He also gave us teaching on how to live a victorious life. (Phil. 4:11,12) Today we have another Paul who can teach many through his book which is so needed in this hour of turmoil and stress. He is a man who has lived through some of these areas, but has learned the freedom of things that controlled his life. I recommend this book, How to Overcome Anger, Bitterness, and Unforgiveness written by Rev. Paul Tribus Th.M., very highly."

Rev. Elvina E. Miller, D.D., Founder & President, The Oasis of Love Church, Shippensburg, Pennsylvania

"This book is a book of hope and healing. I find it to be sound Bible teaching and was very moved by reading it. It opened my eyes in these critical areas, and I highly recommend this book. Read how to be an overcomer, not a casualty."

Dr. Anne Gimenez, President, International Women In Leadership, Co-Pastor, Rock Church, Virginia Beach, Virginia

"I know no better time for such a book as this, and no better person to address these issues than Reverend Paul Tribus. He shares from his personal experiences as a Veteran, a pastor, and a counselor. My hope and prayer is that many will find peace through the pages of this book and in the process become acquainted with the Prince of Peace."

Bishop John Gimenez, Rock Ministerial Fellowship, Co-Pastor, Rock Church, Virginia Beach, Virginia

"Anger, bitterness, and unforgiveness have not gone away. Paul Tribus describes how these emotions can erode Christian character. How to Overcome Anger, Bitterness, and Unforgiveness

is a balanced, Bible based guide around the pitfalls of life—a must for every Christian."

Dr. David Minor Sr., Senior Pastor, Gospel Tabernacle, Coudersport, Pennsylvania

"'How to' books are not usually on my reading list, but because Pastor Tribus is my friend I read his book. To my great surprise it was filled with real answers and insightful applications to some of today's most pressing problems. Good humor is sprinkled throughout the book! I'm sure you will enjoy reading it and be blessed by his insight."

Rev. Vinny Losciale, Senior Pastor, Beach Fellowship, Virginia Beach, Virginia

"As humanity continues to be broiled in the stew of relational conflict, it is heartening to read personal and practical strategies for overcoming life's dilemmas. Pastor Tribus has applied scripture to address critical areas of need. Is it advisable to utilize his approach to resolving anger and bitterness? In my opinion, the sooner...the better."

Rev. David Dillon, Senior Pastor, Rock Church, Franklin, Virginia

"This is a powerful message from a writer who has seen life from the bottom up. It is not just 'lip-service' to these important issues, but the truth from experience."

Chuck Dean, Author, *Nam Vet — Making Peace with Your Past*

"As a pastor and in ministry for over 40 years, of the many things people have to deal with, I have found anger, bitterness and unforgiveness, to be the top three. In a straightforward and 'plain English' style, Paul deals with these important problems. Read and chew on this book…it will help to change your life and guide you in helping others as well. I highly recommend this reading."

Dr. B. J. Pruitt, Founder/Chairman, Mission Teams International

"From one Marine to another, this book is powerful in combat. Anger, bitterness and unforgiveness, are enemies that attack our lives, and family, on a daily basis. Paul Tribus, in his Marine style, has located these strongholds of the enemy, and has attacked them head on. I march with Paul on this assault against the enemy's ambush."

Bishop Val Melendez, Soul Saving Station, Ahoskie, North Carolina

"After reviewing this book, I have asked that it be translated into several other languages so we can us it in India. All over the

world people are facing the same problems, and we need this kind of teaching. I am going to ask all our pastors, and teachers here in India to read this book by Pastor Paul Tribus."

Rev. John Lazarus, Rock Churches/India

CONTENTS

DEDICATION

To all the victims of anger, bitterness and unforgiveness. May this book help you to no longer be a victim, but an overcomer. May God grant you the courage to get in the fight of faith and recover all the time and energy you have spent in these areas. The enemy of your soul, the devil, would have you be a slave to anger, bitterness and unforgiveness, but you can be set free and know the true love of God.

Acknowledgments

I would like to personally acknowledge all the people, places and circumstances that have brought me to this present day. Thank God for the good, the bad and the ugly. As I begin to see God's hand upon my life, I can see that even my stumbling blocks can be turned into stepping stones. Where you are weak, He can be strong. We are chosen vessels, yet earthen vessels. May we always remember to keep a tender heart towards the Lord and lean upon Him for help.

A great big "thank you" to my wife Joanne, my son Michael and my daughter Michele, who have stood by my side these many years. We are "super-strugglers" in life.

FOREWORD

I have known Paul Tribus for a number of years and have found him to be an honest, sincere and upright man. These traits are vitally important when a person sits down to write a book. Is this person speaking the truth? Are his comments derived from a theoretical base or does he communicate from experience?

May I urge you to read Paul's thoughtful words slowly and carefully. They are sure to have a positive effect on your life and view of the future. With sincere anticipation of your betterment I recommend this publication to you.

James Lee Beall, Bethesdsa Christian Church, Sterling Heights, Michigan

INTRODUCTION

Anger, bitterness and unforgiveness are real problems in this world today. Many people wrestle with these areas and spend much of their time struggling with them. The roots of these problems are often deep-seated, touching our emotions and spirit.

These problems are around you everyday. You work with people or meet them in grocery stores or banks—people who live with anger, bitterness and unforgiveness. Whether they deal with them themselves, or someone in the family struggles, they affect the family and those close to you. They affect decisions and lifestyles everyday. Your actions are a result of what is inside. If you never deal with anger, bitterness or unforgiveness, they will rob you of your full potential in life. They will eat at you, and you will become very self-centered. There will be resentment towards others, which need not be. They will eventually control all you do.

As you look closer into these areas, I ask that you open up your heart to God and His Word. Be honest and open to deal in the areas that need help. This book is not to condemn you or criticize you, but to release you into the freedom God wants for you. It will also offer you insight into real, down to earth problems that plague our society and the church today.

I am going to unveil some of the enemy's plot to rob you of your time and potential. The quicker you deal with them, the sooner you will realize the areas in your life that need to be healed. Satan wants to rob you of your time and energy. When something is eating at you inside, it tears you down emotionally and then physically. Your spirit becomes weak, and many people never deal with the problem.

When you go to the doctor, it is because something doesn't feel right. He examines you and makes a diagnosis. You then get medicine or treatment. If you don't go to the doctor, a sickness might become much worse.

When you go to a dentist with a toothache, he takes that drill and goes right to the problem. It hurts for a while, but it must be done. We know that when we go to the dentist, he is not going anywhere but to the pain. However, the pain gets so bad at times, that we will do anything—even hear that annoying drill!

This is also true in dealing with anger, bitterness and unforgiveness. Like a cancer, they eat away at our soul and spirit. You must go to the root and dig it out.

I have seen all three of these things in my life at one time or another. I also know that they can be overcome with the help of God and a willing heart. I have also seen others who are not open to see these in their life and are being destroyed because of them. The enemy wants to keep us self-centered and likes it when we entertain these thoughts of self-pity and resentment.

nil –

When you allow anger, bitterness and unforgiveness to rule your life, it hurts you—and those around you. Listen to some of the words of those who struggle in anger, bitterness and unforgiveness, yet denial. "It's my life, and I'll live it the way I want to." "You just don't know what they did to me." "They deserve everything they get." "She pushed me to hit her; it was all her fault." "These kids push me to get mad." "No one appreciates all I do for them." These are all excuses, yet signs that there is something wrong. Do you see yourself somewhere in here? Do you see your spouse, or friend? Whether yourself, or a friend, or a spouse, this book will offer help to expose anger, bitterness and unforgiveness, and give answers to help.

Now, let me introduce myself to you. I want you to know me so you will open your heart to God. My name is Paul Andrew Tribus. I have a wife and two children, all of whom I am well pleased. I have been in full-time ministry for over twenty-two years. Everything I learn is not necessarily from books but from life experiences.

When I was eighteen years old, I joined the Marine Corps. I served in Vietnam as a machine gunner with the 26th Marines. I have faced the problems of anger, bitterness and unforgiveness in life and in ministry. What I will share with you in this book are some practical and some spiritual ways to deal with these problems. I have seen the Holy Spirit work in my life to overcome in these areas.

There is hope as you ask God to help. An overcomer is one who *is* overcoming. I try to learn from the Holy Spirit, and from my mistakes. Also, we learn from others who have walked the same path. I have worked hard to study these problems and draw from my experiences to help you overcome anger, bitterness and unforgiveness.

This book only covers a small portion and deserves much more study. However, it has enough ammunition to fight a good fight and become a winner in the arena of life.

1

Anger

The phone was ripped from the wall; plants that you cared for are now scattered all over the kitchen floor. Your favorite vase for cut flowers is smashed in pieces. The kids hear the arguing and see the same man who smiles in church on Sunday, now throwing a fit in the home. Sound familiar? Believe it or not, this scene happens more often that we think, even in good Christian homes. These things need not to be happening; but how do you stop? "My temper gets the better of me." "I promise to control myself." "I'll never do it again." "Please forgive me." You hear these words time and time again, yet the explosions still take place. You either control that temper or it will control you. It's not good enough to have it controlled for a while. Your temper will set fear into others, not knowing what will set you off next.

Anger weakens a man and puts him at a disadvantage in life. Anger blurs the visual centers of the brain and will cause physical, as well as spiritual damage. When a man becomes angry, his respiration deepens, the heart beats more rapidly, blood pressure rises, blood rushes to the heart and the central nervous system. Sugar is freed from the liver, the spleen contracts, and adrenaline is secreted.

Anger is not an argument, but a feeling of displeasure set off in your mind. You've seen the results of your anger, and you must remember how you feel after your fit. It's not worth it, yet people continue to allow their feelings to get the better of them. You must realize that anger is used to play into the hands of the enemy. The Bible teaches us to be angry, but sin not (Ephesians 4:26). If you find your temper or anger getting the best of you, then it is sin. The way to deal with sin is by first calling it what it is, SIN! Confess it before God and ask Him for help. It must be conquered in your life and that temper must be overcome. You can have the victory through Christ, who gives you the strength.

An angry man is angry all over again with himself when he finally calms down. When anger is out of control to the point of sin, you, along with others, become victims. You play into the hands of the enemy, and the devil uses it to destroy lives and relationships. The word victory comes from two words: *victim* and *story*. You were once a victim, but now you have a story of overcoming. There cannot be a victory without a battle.

Quit blaming others for your anger. It's a mind-set. If someone or some circumstance causes you to become angry, give it to God. Release that part of your life to the Holy Spirit. Declare war in your mind that you will not let anger ruin your life and relationships with others. When your go to bed angry, you have the devil as a bed partner. Learn not to sleep with your enemies. There can be something in your past that has happened to cause you to be angry and has settled in your mind and spirit. You need to look back and ask God to help you find the root. This is not to blame someone or something, but to find the root and deal with it. You may need to forgive a person and release that to God, and go on in life. Forgiveness is an act of the will. Forgetting is a process. You might say, "I cannot control my temper," or "I cannot forgive someone." That is a lie, and the enemy has tricked you into it. No more excuses! Deal with it! It is an act of the will. Simply believe God, and His Word, and not your emotions. It can be done.

I had to look back over my own life and pin point roots in my own spirit that caused anger. I saw the results of anger in my life that would only hurt myself and those close to me. I joined the Marines when I was 18 and was a machine gunner with the 26th Marines. After coming home from Vietnam in 1969, I found myself getting angry, and many times out of control.

As I looked back many years later, I saw that my anger came because I felt I had been mis-used by others. Some anger was deep inside of me because I couldn't understand why some of my best friends were killed in the war and I was allowed to come home. Many, many unanswered questions! It all resulted in anger. I had to face it head-on. I realized that I had a temper that would sometimes get out of control, and I had to confess my sin to God. I may not have had all my questions answered, but I had to trust God that He knows what is best for my life and He knows what He is doing. You suffer greatly when you allow unforgiveness in your life. When you do, you give the enemy an open channel to continue to harass you. It's not worth it. It's never too late. Sometimes you are angry for lost years, or time lost. Life is too short to allow our enemies to control us. You will find that many people are physically sick because they refuse to face their own sin. You constantly blame others and fail to have the victory. This could change for you right now. Recognize the sin in your life and have a mind-set to deal with it, head-on.

> *"You suffer greatly when you allow unforgiveness in your life. When you do, you give the enemy an open channel to continue to harass you."*

Pray with me. *"Lord, I confess that I have a problem with anger and unforgiveness. From this time on I will not blame others, but take full blame for myself. I release to you all the guilt. I forgive those who have hurt me in their words and actions. I ask you to help me to be gentle and kind, and for you to make me strong in my spirit and my mind to trust you. I have sinned and ask you to forgive me. I will look to you when I start to feel those feelings that in times past have made me sin. I know you can and will help me and I will submit myself to the principles of your Word, and to your Holy Spirit. Help me, dear Lord, to recognize the sin in my own life so I may learn to repent quickly. The devil is my enemy, and no one else. He rejoices every time I fall; but I thank God that Jesus is on my side as I decide to serve God. I will study your Word and yield my heart to serve you. Forgive me, Lord, for those I have hurt;. and I will use every opportunity to take full blame when I see them to ask their forgiveness. This I pray in Jesus' name. I thank you that this is a new day for me. Amen."*

2

Get Help!

Several years ago I was home for supper, about ready to sit down and eat when the phone rang. "Pastor, I need you here right away; there is a serious problem." Well, you know us pastors; I had to go. I hurried to the lady's house. She was new in the church, and I really wanted to be there for her. I remember knocking at the door, she opened the door and I walked in and sat on the sofa. I asked, "What is the problem?" She then pointed to the kitchen, and out walked her husband. You know the scene. It was only then that I noticed the broken furniture, the plants thrown across the room, and a fist put through the wall. I felt so helpless and awkward. All I really wanted to do was get out of there. I looked at the door to make my exit. It was here I learned I am not everyone's answer in the church. I did manage to calm him down, and prayed with them.

What does one do with situations like this? Well, let me give you some advice from experience. Call the police! I came to the conclusion that the police are also God's ministers. Didn't know that, did you? Well, they are. They are in authority to protect us, and we must recognize them as such. Now, I'm not telling you to call the police for every problem; but there are times to do it. Not all of God's angels wear white. Some of them wear blue and their phone number is 911.

In the multitude of council there is wisdom. Talk to a minister of the Gospel or a good Christian counselor who will advise you. Don't feel like you are doing wrong in getting help. Someone might say you'll embarrass them; but if a man strikes his wife, he is harming her and is not being the Christian husband God told him to be. You say, "He's always been this way." Well, now you both really need help and counseling to get this thing right.

When you are dealing with an angry or bitter person, he must be made aware of his problem. Ask him to get some help, and then follow up. Be sure they are following through and not just going through the motions. There is a serious problem, and it must be dealt with to the root.

> *"When you are dealing with an angry or bitter person, he must be made aware of his problem."*

There have been certain problems I have dealt with in children where medication was needed. This could possibly be so in some cases, but most of it is a learned behavior that must be controlled and overcome. Deal with it. Sooner or later it will become a more serious problem, and you will have wished you would have done something about it earlier.

The Bible teaches us how the older woman should teach the younger. One thing we are missing in our generation is "getting together." I don't mean just getting together for a meeting, but the way they used to. Years ago the women would get together and cook, or can fruit. They would share and help each other with children and home life. Now-a-days the wife has to handle it all by herself. In many areas, she just doesn't know what to do.

When a woman has to go to work with bruises over her arms and face because her husband beats her—it is too late. In most cases the abuse didn't start out like that, but the problem just got bigger and bigger. Now she's afraid to tell someone for fear of what he will do, physically or mentally.

In most cases abuse starts verbally. This is the early stage of anger or bitterness beginning to rear its ugly head. The problem is already there, and the root must be dealt with. There is absolutely no reason for a man to strike a woman, and he needs to get help. Get good help. Get help from someone who knows God and His Word. Then the wife needs some support, with encouragement and building back the respect she has lost for herself.

If you ask of God bread, He will not give you a stone. If you come to God honestly and ask for help, He will give it. First go to Him in prayer and repentance. He will bring the right people to help you through. The fact is, you do need help, and it is nothing to be embarrassed about. Think of the times of embarrassment you put your wife and kids through—the self-respect they have lost and the confidence in facing life. Just denying it, or burying it, is not the answer. It's like covering up a cancer with a bandage. It is inside a root. Just to be sorry is not enough. A good minister or counselor will guide you to God's Word and help you personally in your needs. It can be overcome through the help of God.

3

Let's Deal

Prisons are full of people who could not control their temper. You say, "That only happens to the other guy." Well, look again, because it can happen. Better yet, it can happen to you, or someone in your household. Perhaps you have always wanted to have a prison ministry. Well, you will have one if you pray asking for it and then do nothing about your life patterns. You'll have plenty of opportunity to minister to prisoners, because you will be one of them. Domestic violence and abuse is serious stuff, and you need to deal with it immediately.

The Bible says in Matthew 5:22: *"But I say unto you, that whosoever is angry with his brother without a cause, shall be in danger of the judgment: and whosoever shall say to his brother, Raca, shall be in danger of the council: but whosoever shall say, thou fool, shall be in danger of hell fire."* Now notice the progression: from your anger being out of control, it could lead to you being in trouble with the council. That is with the law or civil authority. Ultimately it controls you to the point of an explosion in your spirit so that you are in danger of going to hell. I'd say that was quite serious.

This is how it happens. People never take it seriously and let anger control them to the point that people kill each other over matters that do not matter at all. Over the years, I've heard of one man killing another because he pulled in front of him at a car wash. Is it worth it? One man killed a younger man who drove a little too slow on the highway. The younger one pulled the older man off the road and began to swing at him, and the older man pulled out a gun and killed him. A young man dead at 18, while they try to figure out why the older man killed him! Was it justified? All this because someone could not control their anger. When it is out of control, you may hurt someone, or you might get killed yourself.

When something starts getting you angry, stop yourself and think, *Is it worth it?* It is better to just walk away. You have nothing to prove, nothing to lose, and everything to gain. It's time to grow up and let that other person cool down a little.

At Kenyan College, the Speech Research Unit did a test that proves when a person is shouted at, he or she cannot help but shout back. The scientific experiment showed that you can keep another person from becoming angry by the tone of your voice. Psychology has proved that if you keep your voice soft you will not become angry. Psychology has accepted as scientific the old Bible injunction, *"A soft answer turneth away wrath"* (Proverbs 15:1). Not only can you keep someone else from becoming angry, but if you practice the principle you will also learn that when you feel yourself becoming angry, do not raise your voice. It will also turn away the wrath in you.

You say, "I can't do that." Oh, yes, you can. It is a mind-set. Start working on it. Tell yourself that next time you feel your temper getting out of control, you will not raise your voice. You will learn to speak softly. See, the whole thing is control. Ask God to help you. You need to be God-controlled, not controlled by your feelings or emotions. Keep cool. Anger is not an argument.

You need to look back at your life and see the things that caused you to become angry. Anger usually is a sign of a shortcoming or lack in your life. Sometimes pride makes this difficult to see. Many times you think you have no lack, but God sees differently. Notice the Laodicean church, in Revelation 3:14-18. They thought they were rich and needed nothing. However, God said they were wretched, miserable, poor, blind, and naked. Quite a difference, wasn't it?

How could someone be so far off? "PRIDE". It hides the true self. The Bible goes on to say to buy gold tried in the fire. In order for gold to be purified, it must be melted down. That takes a lot of heat. Anyone can lose his temper and strike back. Hey, that's easy to do. But God wants you to control your spirit. Proverbs 16:32 says, *"He that is slow to anger is better than the mighty; and he that ruleth his spirit than he that taketh a city."* When things get hot, let the Lord scrape all those impurities that rise to the surface. Don't hide them and let them harden in you. See, the purer the gold, the softer and more pliable it is. You don't just want to look good, but we want to be pure before God. The Bible tells us to buy the truth. Remember this, that every ounce of truth will cost you a pound of flesh. This is how you buy truth: not with dollars, but by bringing your flesh under control.

> *"Remember this, that every ounce of truth will cost you a pound of flesh. This is how you buy truth: not with dollars, but by bringing your flesh under control."*

Anger not only shows a shortcoming or weakness, but it makes you do ridiculous or harmful acts. You say things to harm or wound another's spirit. Many times you go back and say you are sorry for what you said. However, you have a heart problem, not a mouth problem. Out of the abundance of the heart, the mouth speaks. You try to cover up the act or the words, but is has to do with the heart. Expose your weakness to God and ask Him to help you. It is also good to have a friend or minister to know an area you are dealing with in being angry, to help pray and encourage you in God's way. Proverbs 19:11 says, *"The discretion of a man deferreth his anger; and it is his glory to pass over a transgression."* Don't let these things bother you. Make up your mind ahead of time not to let it get to you. Let it pass over. It's not worth it. Remember the results. You can conquer anger in your flesh and be a glory to God, or you can let anger control you and look and act like a fool. *"Be not hasty in thy spirit to be angry, for anger resteth in the bosom of fools"* (Ecclesiastes 7:9).

Now, in place of that anger you need to be kind and tenderhearted. This takes practice, and you need to work on it. Plan to be nice and kind ahead of time. Drive that anger out of your life and replace it with doing good. *"Let all bitterness and wrath and anger and clamor and evil speaking be put away from you, with all malice: and be ye kind one to another, tenderhearted, forgiving one another, even as God for Christ's sake hath forgiven you"* (Ephesians 4:31-32).

"Be angry and sin not: let not the sun go down upon your wrath. Neither give play to the devil" (Ephesians 4:26-27). Learn to deal quickly with anger that results in sin. Don't let it sit for days or weeks before you try to make things right. The Bible is telling you to deal with it now, no matter how much of a fool you have made of yourself.

Several years ago I was at a basketball game where my son was playing. It was a small gym that had very little room, even for fans. The referee had made several calls that I disagreed with, and I said something, not realizing how easy it was for him to hear me. At half-time the referees did not go into a separate room, but they sat across the gym, and his eye caught my eyes. He looked at me and said something stupid. I went off!! I jumped up from my seat and ran across the gym floor right to him. Everything in me wanted to hit or kick him. I told him I didn't appreciate what he said and everyone watched—my son, his friends, the teachers, the coaches, EVERYONE!

One of the coaches restrained me, and I told him what happened. He walked with me back to my seat as the second half of the game started. Now I was angry at myself sitting there the whole second half of the game, thinking what a fool I made of myself. I'm a Christian. I'm a minister. What should I do? My heart then started to melt before the Spirit of God. I began to think how easy I became angry and could have hurt him; or he, me. The devil began to condemn me. How foolish I was; and it was easy to just go back to those old ways.

I had been doing so well; how did this happen? Then I remembered a verse of scripture; "*Agree with thine adversary quickly*" (Matthew 5:25). So I quickly told the devil that he was right—I blew it, but he wasn't going to have the victory. As soon as the game was over, I immediately went to that referee and told him how sorry I was. He looked me square in the eye and said he was sorry, too. We shook hands and I began to walk away.

As I walked away, the Spirit of God spoke to my heart to go back and tell him who I was. Boy, I thought about that for a second, then rebuked the devil and kept walking. Again, the Lord touched my heart to go back to him. This was hard. But I thought God was dealing with me to humble myself, so I went back to him. "I'm an ordained minister and a pastor of a church," I said. He again looked at me and tears came to his eyes. "I'm the head referee of the whole league" he said, and "I'm here training other referees how to handle games and fans." He further told me he was an elder in his church, and that he lied to me about what he said, because he really said it. He asked me to forgive him; I asked him to forgive me; and everyone watched as we cried, hugged and prayed together.

What could have been a complete disaster turned out to be a real lesson. What had set it all off? My mouth! Just a few simple words of sarcasm, telling him he was making some bad calls. I learned something from all that. I try to be more careful in situations like that, and if I ever make a mistake I'm quick to deal with it.

Listen to the words of Theodore Roosevelt.

"The credit belongs to the man who is actually in the arena, who's face is marred by dust and sweat and blood, who strives valiantly; who errs and comes short again and again, who knows the great enthusiasms, the great devotions, and spends himself in a worthy cause, who at the best knows the triumph of high achievement and how, at the worst, if he fails at least fails while daring greatly, so that his place shall never be with those cold and timid who know neither victory nor defeat."

Now let's get the job done and deal with that anger. Stick with it, even if you struggle at first, but work on it. Practice these principles; and with God's help, it can be done.

"I can do all things through Christ which strengtheneth me" (Philippians 4:13).

39

4

How to be Yourself

God is Love. He is love and will not change. This is reliable. However, you will never be secure in that love until you trust Him. When you begin to trust God, you discover your security is in God and not in yourself. God made you and He has a purpose for you. In today's world, it is easy to lose a sense of identity. You become a number in society, and you try to fit into some mold. You must come to the understanding that God accepts you the way you are. You will have a freedom in your emotions and know that God knows your personality. When you come to that realization, you can dare to be yourself—in all circumstances.

If you do not like yourself and do not come to the understanding that God accepts you, you will begin to be developed by others. The world system will begin to mold you. You will seek approval somewhere. You begin to look for rewards somewhere, and this will lead to problems because you will never out grow your old nature of selfishness.

Peer pressure drives you to become someone you were never meant to be, and the last stages are worse than the beginning. Now you find yourself in a deep rut and dig yourself in deeper. To change, you need to start by digging yourself out. It's strange, but you took quite a time to get into this problem, and yet you want to be out immediately. It all starts with a decision—a mind-set. I need to change and be the person God made me to be. God doesn't take away all your desires, but He re-channels them. You need to motivate yourself towards God and being a helpful part of this world.

In re-channeling your energies towards God, you are helped in correcting the wrong patterns you have learned and replace them with new ones. In doing this, it will create a self-acceptance and self respect. When you do, you realize your existence and being in terms of God's love, and not man's acceptance.

It is not an easy road, because there will be circumstances and people who will challenge you. However, as you study scriptures, you will find many of the people that

God used had every reason to have poor self-respect. It takes trust and faith in God to step out into the acceptance of God's love. If you don't, you will continue to blame others for your low self esteem, or blame circumstances on how life was unfair to you. You can no longer look to the world or to people for praise or acceptance. Your source must be God and His Word. Only as you do this can you truly accept who you are, and realizing that if the world or people accepts or rejects you is not the most important thing. You need to plunge into the love and acceptance of God's love.

When you come to God honestly and openly, it always brings peace. Many times you continue to suffer from the pain of guilt or condemnation long after you have dealt with the problem. These are your emotions reacting to things not related to your problem. This is false guilt and wrong thinking or wrong information. You must have trust in God's Word that when you come to God and ask forgiveness, you receive it. You must not condemn yourself. David asked God to deliver him from blood-guiltiness. This means that you can add nothing to God's forgiveness. You cannot earn merit with God by works. Simply, believe God! God will send His peace into the troubled areas of your mind and emotions.

Sometimes you are trying to live up to standards set up by others that are unrealistic, or you put demands upon yourself because of someone you want to be like. When your feelings and emotions begin to condemn you, you must turn to God with confidence that He will free you in every area. Philippians 1:6 says, *"Being confident of this very thing,*

43

that he which hath begun a good work in you will perform it until the day of Jesus Christ."

> *"When your feelings and emotions begin to condemn you, you must turn to God with confidence that He will free you in every area."*

In finding the true love of God, you will be content and satisfied in who you are and what God is doing in you. Paul tells us in Philippians 4:11-12, *"Not that I speak in respect of want: for I have learned, in whatsoever state I am, therewith to be content. I know both how to be abased, and I know how to abound. Everywhere and in all things I am instructed both to be full and to be hungry, both to abound and to suffer need."*

Sometimes you expect too much of yourself in this life, or you expect too much out of life. You must learn to adjust your inner self to be content in the task God has for you. It is unwise to compare yourself with others. (You seem to always determine your "insides" by what you see of others' "outsides"). When you look into the mirror, you must be content and happy with the creation of God. Tell yourself you are God's and that God did not make a mistake. Take off the spiritual mask you sometimes wear to impress others with. Be open with God and ask Him to help you grow and mature. God wants to see you grow and realizes you will make some mistakes along the way. Be confident that God understands and He loves you.

5

Bitterness

Bitterness, unlike anger, is more difficult to detect. Anger can be denied for a time, but there are explosions and visible or audible reactions. Bitterness is deep-seated in the emotions and is like a cancer. Offenses that are not resolved harden in the heart and turn to bitterness. It causes one to be resentful and to have deep pain over an offense that was not dealt with. Hebrews 12:13-14 says, *"Follow peace with all men, and holiness, without which no man shall see the Lord: Looking diligently lest any man fail of the grace of God lest any root of bitterness springing up trouble you, and thereby many be defiled".*

Bitterness starts as a root, and spreads. You will find yourself seeking those who take up the offense with you. This often causes "clicks" to form against a person or group. Often the whole story is never known.

Nothing can tear up a fellowship or church quicker than spreading criticism born out of bitterness. It doesn't show up as anger. It is often passive, or even out of seemingly genuine and great concern. However, it spreads like poison and is very dangerous if not dealt with. This is why the Bible gives clear understanding in dealing with this.

Whenever you hear, or become aware of, an offense, whether from the source or someone else, ask if Biblical procedures were followed. If there is an offense with a person, ask him if he went to that person to bring peace to the situation. *You* can become part of something very ugly if you are not careful! You find yourself right in the middle of something that wasn't even your problem in the first place. Learn to mind your own business. Proverbs 26:17 says, *"He that passeth by, and meddleth with strife belonging not to him, is like one that taketh a dog by the ears."*

"Open rebuke is better than secret love" (Proverbs 27:5). Correct a wise man, and he will be wiser. If someone is really desiring to follow the Lord and be right, they will heed your advice. If he doesn't, you will be glad you didn't become part of that problem. Keep in mind that you are dealing with bitterness. Deal with that rather than hurting the person. Let him know in love that it is not worth it and that he is big enough to handle the problem. Let him know you have confidence in him to bring the offense out in the open to the offender, not to everyone. Then if that

person doesn't listen, take someone with you. This is Bible pattern. God will be well pleased as you give no place to the devil.

Give that offense and bitterness to God. Now is the time to make up your mind to do something about your life and about the issues in your life. If you feel that energy being drained from your life, and you know deep within your own heart that you need healing, then now is the time. If you feel that no one cares or sees the death you are dying, it's time. It's time for you to make that move, and press through every thought, every obstacle and every spiritual enemy, and touch Jesus. He is there to release His power into your spirit and into your life. It is not time for self-pity and for expecting everyone to come running to you. Jesus doesn't make an issue of your problem; why should you? Remember, people don't see the wounds deep within their mind and in their spirit. But Jesus sees, and He waits for you to do something about it. Now is your time; press through.

This is what you do with bitterness. Press through to "Doctor" Jesus. There are some situations that have been in you for years. Possibly the offender has died or moved away. Ask God to help you as He wants to restore you to health.

Twice in my life I have seen a man severely beaten: once when I was in the service and once after I became a pastor. In both cases the person's face was marred and swollen so badly that he was unable to see.

As a Christian, I know that Jesus was beaten, too. But as He lay in the tomb and the grubs came to eat off His flesh, something miraculous happened. He received a healing from the Father. After the resurrection He still had the scars in his hands, feet and side; but there is no record of any signs of the beatings. He was no longer disfigured.

You may feel as if your life has been ruined by beatings. You may be convinced that no one cares about you. Maybe you feel that you barely exist in a place of death and that there is no hope for you. If that is your situation, regardless of what you believe about Jesus right now, consider what it could mean for you to come back to life again as a whole person, without a trace of disfigurement. You may always have a few scars; after all, they confirm what you have gone through. But those scars have no power to hurt you. They can become scars of healing, to be shared with others.

> *"You may always have a few scars; after all, they confirm what you have gone through. But those scars have no power to hurt you. They can become scars of healing, to be shared with others."*

Whatever your offenses or hurts may be, if you want to turn your life around, the most important step you can take is to believe in the Jesus of the tomb.

Bitterness only hurts you. You are letting an offense, no matter how severe, to eat at your spirit and deprive you of peace and joy. It is possible for you to deal with it and ask God for help. Put aside all personal pride, and face it head-on. You will experience a freedom you have never known. You will know a peace that passes all human understanding. The devil wants you to stay in the rut that you have dug yourself into. It doesn't matter what anyone else thinks. You be the first one to deal with it. Go to God, and then to anyone else you have to in order to make it right. It is not important what kind of response you get, but what you do. It will clear your own heart. Someone else might not even know there was an offense or problem. You are doing what God wants you to do, and you will experience the release of that bitterness. Jesus does good work.

There is a story in the Bible in Matthew 9:20-22 where Jesus healed a woman with an issue of blood. Twelve years she sought for help, spending all her money in her search for health.

From the Mosaic law we learn that anyone with an issue of blood is unclean. Even a man with an running issue is unclean. Now remember, not only is that person unclean, but anyone he or she comes in contact with, is unclean. The Word of the Lord also teaches us that the life is in the blood; therefore, people who bleed are seeing their very life drained out of them. So as we look at this woman in Matthew 6:20-22, we see that she has a very limited relationship with her family, has no friends, is weak physically and is drained emotionally, spiritually and financially. Now we begin to see a little deeper into what really happened.

Jesus came walking by, and this woman, in desperation, pressed through the crowd and touched the hem of His garment. Jesus stopped and asked, "Who touched me?" Can you imagine, with thousands of people around Him, that He would ask such a question? But something had happened in the spirit, that no one physically saw.

I can see that woman knowing that something had happened to her. For the first time in twelve years she felt such a rush of life and strength because this issue became clean in her life. Within her own mind there was an emotional release, to know she would have a full relationship with her husband and could embrace her children. Oh, what a moment of great joy she experienced because she pressed through to touch Jesus, the great Healer. No one else in the crowd realized that anything had happened.

Perhaps you have an issue that is draining the very life out of you. It affects not only you, but also others with whom you come in contact. For years I did not realize that someone could hemorrhage internally and die. You cannot see any external bleeding. Now, spiritually, you can die from an issue in your life that is draining you spiritually and emotionally. You need to be healed. Only Jesus can heal that wound. You must press through the circumstances of life to touch Jesus and have His power released into your spirit. You will never be the same. You have lived with that issue long enough; it has cost you time and energy and affected others around you. It is time to press through.

Now is the time to make up your mind to do something about your life and about the issues in your life. If you feel that energy being drained from your life, and you know deep within your own heart that you need healing, then now is the time. If you feel that no one cares or sees the death you are dying, it's time. It's time for you to make that move, and press through every thought, every obstacle and every spiritual enemy and touch Jesus. He is there to release His power into your spirit and into your life. It is not a time for self-pity and for expecting everyone to come running to you. Jesus doesn't make an issue of your problem; why should we? Remember, we don't see the wounds deep within your mind and in your spirit. But Jesus sees, and He awaits for you to do something about it. Now is your time; press through.

6

Unforgiveness

A little boy, when asked what forgiveness is, gave this answer: "It is the smell of a flower when they are trampled upon." That says a lot. What kind of odor do you give off when you are trampled upon? How about the cross?

In this life you will have opportunity to exercise forgiveness. The Bible says that offenses will come (Luke 17:1). When people get offended with one another, the situation needs immediate attention, or the matter can get worse. That unforgiveness can grow into bitterness and affect others. The Bible says, *"Great peace have they which love thy law: and nothing shall offend them"* (Psalm 119:165).

Anyone who gets offended easily, and often doesn't love the Word of God very much. He should read and love God's Word and know these things will happen in life.

To truly forgive someone you must know that God has forgiven you. God's forgiveness is a fact. You must simply accept His forgiveness and forgive yourself. This is not based on emotion or whether you feel it or not; it is fact. God has forgiven you all your trespasses and has totally forgiven you. Now you must apply that to your life and walk in that peace and assurance. If you have any doubt about that, let's stop right here and ask God to forgive you. Ask the Holy Spirit to witness to your spirit that God loves you and accepts you. Confess your need for forgiveness and simply receive it.

We now must learn to forgive others. *"For if ye forgive men their trespasses, your heavenly Father will also forgive you: But if ye forgive not men their trespasses, neither will your Father forgive your trespasses"* (Matthew 6:14-15). When you do not forgive men their trespasses, you are enslaved to the darkness of unforgiveness. You will find yourself trying to ignore the matter or trying to concentrate on other things, hoping the issue will go away. Then you start to blame others for the offense.

True forgiveness is an act of the will, not the emotions. You need to know it is your choice either to forgive that person or be a slave to unforgiveness for quite some time.

> *"True forgiveness is an act of the will, not the emotions. You need to know it is your*

> *choice either to forgive that person or be a slave to unforgiveness for quite some time.*"

There are different types of offenses and different ways to handle the matter.

☐ **The offense is unaware.** Sometimes people or circumstances offend you and the person is truly unaware what has happened. I received a call a while back from a man who told me I offended him about 15 years previously. He went on to say that he decided to forgive me and release me. I prayed with him and said that all was well and to go on and serve the Lord. This was an offense I was not even aware of. He should have come to me a long time ago and asked me if I knew that I offended him. What you should do in these cases is simply take it to God and leave it at the cross.

There was another circumstance in my life where I was offended with someone. This brother told someone to come and talk to me about something I had done. However, he did not have all the facts, and I was offended because people jumped to conclusions. Man, I was hot. I went to find the brother and told him how I felt. He simply told me he was very busy at the time and just told someone else to get a message to me—he didn't even have an attitude about it. Well, as he humbled himself I felt very foolish. Someone once said, "Keep your words soft and sweet because you may have to eat them." The matter was resolved and life went on. These are learning experiences that help us all get through life. There are things in your life that bother you about what someone has said or done. Possibly that person is unaware of any offense. Just drop the matter. You are the one that is making it a problem. Take it to God and leave it.

☐ **You are the offender.** In this situation you realize somewhere you caused some offense. Possibly through prayer or another circumstance you see something in your own heart that has hurt someone else. A simple phone call, or knowing the next time you see that person you will ask for forgiveness, should be enough. When you ask for forgiveness, establish it beforehand that you are going to take the blame for your actions. Do not wait for the other person to apologize or repent. Sometimes that doesn't happen. You go and make it right; otherwise your asking for forgiveness is based on conditions. If that person does not forgive you, then it is now their problem, not yours.

Humbling yourself is the key. You'll be surprised at the people that come into my office and say, "I'll forgive them if they forgive me." They are missing the whole picture. When you are the offender, simply own up and ask forgiveness for your actions in a given situation. The results may take some time, but it must be settled in your heart that your part is done. You don't have to beg or punish yourself. If that person never forgives you, it is not your problem. If that person wants to be a martyr and tell everyone about the offense and how terrible you are, let them. The pain may not go away for a while, but the situation is in God's hands. Remember, in all types of offenses and forgiveness the principle is releasing it to God. He is the judge, not you. Humble yourself, and in due time God will lift you up. Trust God that these are principles that do work.

□ **You have been offended.** In this situation something has happened that offended you and you are having a problem with it. First of all, pray, because possibly you are just over-tired or let something bother you that usually never does. The Bible is clear that you need to go to the person that caused the offense. If you do this, you could save a lot of problems later. Now your approach to that person should not be one of pre-determined guilt. Always give someone the benefit of the doubt until the whole matter is brought out into the open. If the offense is serious enough, only then should you take someone else to help resolve the matter. Ultimately your trust is in God. When you have done these things, drop the issue and leave it with the Lord.

Now you might ask, "What happens if they just ask for forgiveness; do they go scott free?" As far as you are concerned—"Yes." You must forgive and release everything to God. He is the final judge in all. If you do not forgive, you are only hurting yourself and wanting control. Remember this, that God knows how to handle the situation better than you. In certain offenses, some restitution may be involved, or possibly a crime has been committed. In these more severe and complicated cases, you may need to get some good council in order to do the right thing. There are different sides to every story, and all situations are different. The key in forgiving is to have a humble spirit; and your motive should be to restore.

What a thrill it was the first time someone came to me to ask me to forgive them for something they had done. I let them know that I forgave them, and it was a "done deal." Always remember how much Jesus forgave you compared to what you really deserve.

☐ **Just Checking!** Several years ago a good friend of ours who did missionary work, and was still in ministry, called me for lunch. My wife and I both went over to her house, and she prepared a nice lunch for the three of us. Before we sat down to eat, she said she had something to ask me.

I said, "Sure. . .what's up?"

"Well," she said, "I just wanted to know if everything was okay with us?"

She went on to say that there was no real offense or reason, only that she felt inside that something could be wrong and felt a coldness between us. I told her that everything was fine and that we were just busy about other things, and there was absolutely no problem. We prayed, ate our meal, and continued our friendship in the Lord. Now, if there was a problem or offense; this was the time to talk about it, because she was ready to deal with anything that came up.

Many times people deny any problems, and yet they allow them to continue to bother them. You put up that "fake front" and say, "Oh, nothing is wrong." Confrontation is good if your interest is to make things right and come away praying and letting forgiveness work in your life.

Now don't go around always checking with everyone and always asking if everything is all right. Use wisdom and learn when to go to someone, or how to deal if some-one comes to you. Again, remember how much Jesus for-gave us, learn to forgive others, and be at peace with one another. So the next time someone comes to you, just checking, remember that it could be very important to them; treat them like you would like to be treated if you were going to them, or someone else, which you will be more than likely to do. What you sow, you will reap.

7

Giving Up the Reins

People who do not deal with their anger, bitterness or unforgiveness often want to be in control. There is little trust with others; and they will use people, circumstances, or money to control the situation. I thought it was quite odd that many of the people I know that deal with these problems want to remain in control. It can get quite ugly at times in separation or divorces when control becomes a factor. This is a clear indication that you must give up the reins and give them to the Lord. The true

Spirit of Christ is to be a servant and humble yourself. I've had people tell me, "Well, I have to fight for what is right." That could be true if you truly know what is right. However, the problem you are in could be because of your controlling spirit, and it is not the answer in dealing with control.

Giving up the reins is not easy. You have a lot of years of having your way by controlling, or you have learned to manipulate people and circumstances. To control or manipulate people is a form of witchcraft. You need to pray for the Spirit of Christ to be in control and live a Spirit controlled life. When situations come up in your life, ask the Lord, "How should I handle this?" Learn not to speak or act so quickly.

When I was in the Marine Corps I learned how to react when attacked. I learned to defend myself until it became a reflex. You just do it automatically because that's the way you were taught. Your life depended upon acting quickly. Now that you want to serve the Lord, and do things His way, you need to be re-trained—quick to pray, slower to respond—quick to listen, slower to speak. Weigh your words, don't count them. Learn to act, speak, and respond the way Jesus would. You say, "That's not easy!" No one said it would be easy.

Maintaining control and manipulating others is only demanding to have your own way and self-control. You want to look good to everyone. Consequently, the only time you humble yourself is when you need to look good. You need always to check your motives and keep an honest heart before the Lord. When you keep yourself free from wrong motives and selfish ways, God takes the responsibility for how things look to others. Quit trying to look good and always having your way. God will give you inner strength. Begin to trust Him. Our external behavior always reflects what is on the inside. Too often you are trying to look good on the outside, when God is working from the inside-out. Let God have the reins of your heart, and He will take control and responsibility. It certainly is a lot better than the mess you made.

Do not expect too much all at once. Remember that it took you a long time to behave the way you do, and it takes work to change it. However, it all starts with you making a decision to give the reins to God and be God-controlled. If you are always divided on the inside, it causes nothing but doubt and fear. Now, the decision is this: *"Lord, I'm going to trust you and I give up control. I've made a mess of things and now ask you to help me and take control."*

> *"Do not expect too much all at once. Remember that it took you a long time to behave the way you do, and it takes work to change it. However, it all starts with you making a decision to give the reins to God and be God-controlled."*

You see, making a decision brings all doubt to an end. You have decided to decide. Once this is done, you will have peace as a result. From now on, tell yourself when any questions rise in your mind that the struggle is over. *"I've decided to do it God's way."* Do not put it off until later. Quit trying to make excuses or look for a better time. The time is now. You're not going to have it all together overnight, but the important thing is to decide. Don't be afraid to make a decision because you might fail or make a mistake. Don't depend on others to make the decision for you. This has to be something you do and have a desire to do. Only you know the true state of your heart. To keep on doing your own thing and having your own way is only deceiving you own self. Your anger, bitterness, and unforgiveness cannot be ignored. If left alone they will continue to eat at your emotions and leave you crippled in life.

As you begin to practice this new set of principles in letting God be in control, you will find yourself looking up and out rather than within. Until you make a decision to give God the reins, you are self-centered and focusing inward. Every decision you make and all your motives are for self. Now you begin to look for ways to help others. You find yourself going out of your way to serve and be a blessing. You realize that others need you, and you can help them. You learn the true meaning of giving, and you begin to see change in your heart that is now reaching out to others. It is possible. You realize that this is the work of God and not your own. Therefore, He gets all the glory. People see your good works, but give the glory to God. This is powerful and gives you new strength in the innerman that you never thought was possible. Give Him the reins.

8

Why Bad Things Happen to Good People

In the midst of dealing with yourself and seeing who you really are, and what you should be, you need a clear picture of God and why He does what He does. Unless you have a vivid picture of who God is and how powerful He is, you will always limit Him and what He can do for you, and in you.

For a clearer picture of how awesome God is, read Psalms 147 and 148. Take time to read these scriptures in your devotion time and let the Holy Spirit bring these scriptures to life in you. I am including them here for your sake, to paint a picture of the great God you serve.

Psalm 147:1-20

"Praise ye the Lord: for it is good to sing praises unto our God; for it is pleasant; and praise is comely.

The Lord doth build up Jerusalem: he gathereth together the outcasts of Israel.

He healeth the broken in heart, and bindeth up their wounds.

He telleth the number of the stars; he calleth them all by their names.

Great is our Lord, and of great power: his understanding is infinite.

The Lord lifteth up the meek: he casteth the wicked down to the ground.

Sing unto the Lord with thanksgiving; sing praise upon the harp unto our God:

Who covereth the heaven with clouds, who prepareth rain for the earth, who maketh grass to grow upon the mountains.

He giveth to the beast his food, and to the young ravens which cry.

He delighteth not in the strength of the horse: he taketh not pleasure in the legs of a man.

The Lord taketh pleasure in them that fear him, in those that hope in his mercy.

Praise the Lord, O Jerusalem; praise thy God, O Zion.

For he hath strengthened the bars of thy gates; he hath blessed thy children within thee.

He maketh peace in thy borders, and filleth thee with the

finest of the wheat.

He sendeth forth his commandment upon earth: his word runneth very swiftly.

He giveth snow like wool: he scattereth the hoarfrost like ashes.

He casteth forth his ice like morsels: who can stand before his cold?

He sendeth out his word, and melteth them: he causeth his wind to blow, and the waters flow.

He sheweth his word unto Jacob, his statues and his judgments unto Israel.

He hath not dealt so with any nation: and as for his judgments, they have not known them. Praise ye the Lord."

Psalm 148:1-14

" Praise ye the Lord. Praise ye the Lord from the heavens: praise him in the heights.

Praise ye him, all his angels: praise ye him, all his hosts.

Praise ye him, sun and moon: praise him, all ye stars of light.

Praise him, ye heavens of heavens, and ye waters that be above the heavens.

Let them praise the name of the Lord: for he commanded, and they were created.

He hath also stablished them for ever and ever: he hath made a decree which shall not pass.

Praise the Lord from the earth, ye dragons, and all deeps: Fire, and hail; snow, and vapour; stormy wind fulfilling his word: Mountains, and all hills; fruitful trees, and all cedars: Beasts and all cattle; creeping things, and flying fowl: Kings of the earth, and all people; princes, and all judges of the earth:

*Both young men, and maidens; old men, and children:
Let them praise the name of the Lord: for his name alone
is excellent; his glory is above the earth and heaven.
He also exalteth the horn of his people, the praise of all his
saints; even of the children of Israel, a people near unto
him. Praise ye the Lord."*

Can you imagine that God put the whole universe into motion by His power? Scientists can come up with all these different theories, but God created the universe and keeps everything moving by His power. Think of the earth, the sun, the moon and all the stars—created by God.

The sun is a star and is the closest star to earth. It is about 93,000,000 miles from the earth. A rocket going about 25,000 MPH, or seven miles a second, would take about 152 days to reach the sun from the earth. Now, to reach the next nearest star, going at the same speed, would take 115,000 years to get there. Imagine that! How great God does things! Don't limit Him; He is awesome. The earth is about 8,000 miles in diameter, while the sun is 865,000 miles. There are large stars that are about 1,000 times that of the sun, or have a diameter of about 1 billion miles. No one knows exactly how many stars there are, but on a clear, dark night, a person can see about 3,000 stars. Altogether about 6,000 stars can be seen from the earth. But these are just the brightest stars—the ones visible without a telescope. A telescope with a 3 inch lens can bring about 600,000 stars into view. The largest telescopes make it possible to detect billions of individual stars and more than a billion galaxies. Astronomers believe that these galaxies consist of a total of about 200 billion billion (200,000,000,000,000,000,000) stars. Now suppose that everyone in the world were to count the stars. Each person could count more than 50 billion of them, without the same star being counted twice.

There are stars we haven't ever discovered; and yet the Bible tells us that God created every star and calls them by name. He is an all-powerful God. He is the God of Creation. He is the God who spoke the world into existence and created the seas. He is the God who provided manna in the wilderness and delivered His people by parting the Red Sea. He is the God who created the lightening and thunder and earthquakes. He is the God of all creation and the God of provision.

Now in the midst of all that, Paul the apostle explained to us, in II Cor. 1:1-7, that He is also the God of all comfort. The Word tells us that He comforts us in all our tribulation, or affliction, that we may be able to comfort others which are in trouble. You see, God allows you to be afflicted and go through hard times, so you can help others going through difficult times. Head knowledge is not enough. You must go through some tough times in order to help others. This is why bad things happen to good people.

> *"You see, God allows you to be afflicted and go through hard times, so you can help others going through difficult times. Head*

69

> *knowledge is not enough. You must go through some tough times in order to help others."*

You think that God is punishing you or that you did something wrong. How wrong you are thinking like that! I Peter 4:12 tells us not to think it strange concerning the fiery trial which is to try us, as though some strange thing happened to you. But we are to rejoice because God will bring good out of it. The Bible teaches us to give thanks in all things. You might not thank God for all things, but you can thank Him in all things. All things work together for good. All things are not good, but they work together for good. Are you getting the picture? If God knows every star and is all powerful, don't you think that He knows every problem and weakness you have? No sparrow falls that He doesn't know about. Christ feels what you feel. He knows what you are going through.

There are things you can only learn through experience. No Bible school, or any books, can take the place of what God will teach you through experience. Paul says He learned to be content. He didn't learn that in Bible school or from reading some book. He learned that through the fiery trials. He learned that in prison. He learned that by being stoned. He learned that by the Roman whip. He learned that by being shipwrecked three times. He learned that through hunger, pain, thirst, fasting, cold, and nakedness. He learned how to be content in good times and in the bad. You need to learn how to be content in the hard times, or in the times when you don't even know what's happening. You don't have any problems in the good times, but you need to learn that whatsoever state you are in, to be content, knowing that God is there in all things and in all times.

I remember one of the most difficult times I faced as a minister. Some circumstances came upon me that were very difficult for me to understand. It involved several people, and I realized I had hurt some people and could not understand the pit in my stomach and the pain I felt going through the problems. I cried and prayed, and prayed and cried, and felt the Lord had left me alone in this problem. I literally felt like I was going to die, and even prayed that I would. I could not understand why God didn't deliver me out of that situation.

As I was going through that difficult time, a man came to my home to pray for me. He looked me straight in the eyes and told me that I would be helping others going through the same problem in the future. I sat there with the prophet of God and opened up my heart with him. As he told me those words, I wanted to believe him so much; but the pain was still there. I realized where I had been wrong and prayed for forgiveness. He told me that God forgave me and made everything clear, but I still felt the pain.

I still could not see anything good in all I was feeling and going through. However, I held on to those words of comfort and continued to pray and did my best to get up and face life. Inside I felt worthless and unworthy, but I came to a place one day where "I said, I will trust you, God, even though I don't see the results I want to see or feel the way I want to feel." I found myself helping others going through difficult times, and I felt their pain and really realized the problems were very real in their life. This was happening day after day.

Now, as I look back, I realize what I went through was to help others. We are so self-centered and always waiting to feel good; but it just doesn't happen that way. Sometimes the circumstances are so confusing that we may never see the results we want. But put your trust in God that He will make everything beautiful in His time. It's not always our way, or our time; but put it in the hands of God. He's the God of all comfort. Let Him comfort you, that you might comfort others.

Why is it that when everything turns out the way we like it, only then do we see what God has done? How about the times when it doesn't come out the way you think it should? Did you ever think God was doing something? Why is it that we always have to have the answers? I have learned that I don't always have the answer for myself or for others. You learn to wait and be patient in God. You learn to bring your own spirit under the control of the Holy Spirit and trust God, even when others don't understand what you are going through, or how it looks to others. If I can do all things through Christ, I can go through all things with Christ. Remember, He is with you through the fire. He doesn't deliver you out of the fire, but takes you through the fire. He's already there waiting for you. You must keep your eyes on the Lord and not worry what others think. You cry out, "God, don't you see what I'm going through?" Be of good cheer, He does care, and He does see. You may not feel it now, and you may never feel or see it; but He is there, because He said so. Just believe it and realize that all your worry isn't going to change the situation. God looks upon your heart and wants you to trust Him—no matter what!

9

Stress

Unless you understand stress and know how to deal with it, somehow it can develop into anger. You will experience a certain amount of stress in your life, because it happens when decisions must be made or you are dealing with other people. Stress is simply pressure that is put upon us. David said, in Psalm 4:1, that through distress, or pressure, he was enlarged. That is to say, he matured or grew in wisdom. You must know how much you can take, and stay within that boundary. Stress can produce anxiety and cause tension within and without.

Paul tells us in Phillipians 4:6-8:

"Be careful for nothing; but in every thing by prayer and supplication with thanksgiving let your request be made known unto God.

And the peace of God, which passeth all understanding, shall keep your hearts and minds through Christ Jesus.

Finally, brethren, whatsoever things are true, whatsoever things are honest, whatsoever things are just, whatsoever things are pure, whatsoever things are lovely, whatsoever things are of good report; if there be any virtue, and if there be any praise, think on these things."

He is telling you not to be anxious about anything. The practical way to deal with this is through prayer. He tells you to let God know about it and to talk to Him about it. Learn to talk direct, to God, how you feel. Talk to Him like your Heavenly Father. He understands you more than anyone else. Be specific in your needs and the things that bother you. Don't be religious and think He is impressed with King James language. Talk to Him and be thankful. When you are thankful, it keeps you focused on needs, and not selfish wants. It also keeps you balanced, so you are not critical or negative in your prayer time.

Too much stress can come when you think everything depends on you. It is good to have a responsible attitude, and to stay within your level of stress. However, you need to learn to pace yourself and learn to say, "No." Ask the Lord for wisdom in the amount of responsibility you take on and keep a balance: body, soul, and spirit. In the church and in life you need to learn to work as a team and cooperate with one another. You need to value your co-workers, and see how you can work together to accomplish the work that God wants done.

The apostle Peter learned this lesson. He thought he had to do everything himself and brought upon himself a great deal of stress. In many verses the Bible says how Peter spoke out saying, "Then said Peter," and "Then answered Peter." It wasn't until the day of Pentecost that it says, "and Peter standing up with the eleven." He finally realized that he was part of a team and not a one-man show. You will never be effective in reaching out to others if you shoot our wounded and major on the minors. Instead of being fishers of men, you become keepers of the aquarium.

You can learn a lesson from geese heading south for the winter. Have you ever wondered why they fly in a V formation? Through studies it has been learned that as each bird flaps its wings, it creates an uplift for the bird immediately following. By flying in a V formation, the whole flock adds at lease 70 percent greater flying range than if each bird flew on its own. You need to learn that if you share a common goal or direction, you can make things much easier, depending upon the thrust of one another. Whenever a goose falls out of formation, it quickly feels the extra effort and resistance of being alone, and quickly gets back into formation to once again feel the uplift from the bird in front of it. You need to learn to stay in your formation with those in your fellowship. Whenever you feel alone or need that extra effort, you might look around and quickly get back into formation.

When the lead goose, or the point man, gets tired, he rotates back in the flock; and another takes the point. Even leaders need to delegate and give the harder jobs to others who are responsible to do so. The geese honk to encourage those up front to keep up their speed. You need to learn to encourage those who head up projects in the church or on the job. You don't have to criticize or gossip about someone to bring them down. Learn to encourage and be part of the team. Learn to be a good follower, because someday you may be called upon to lead. What you sow, you will reap. Even if you think you can do a better job, be an encourager. God wants gap fillers, not gap finders. Anyone can sit back and become critical. That's easy. Learn to encourage.

In the Marines we did a lot of drills. I had to learn to march in rank and in step with the whole platoon. If someone was finding it difficult to stay in step, we didn't throw him out of the Marines, but simply put him in the rear of the formation until he learned how to follow. If he was allowed to be in the front, he would cause those in back of him to be out of step. Don't be too bitter when you are asked to step out of the front to the rear. You are not being thrown out—only learning to follow. Humble yourself, as God will exalt you in due season.

Finally, when a goose gets sick, or is wounded and falls out, two geese fall out of formation and follow him to the ground to help and protect him. They stay with him until he is either able to fly, or until he is dead. Only then they fly with another formation flying by, and try to catch up with their original formation. If only you could learn to care for each other like that! You sometimes become so project–minded or goal–oriented that you forget you are part of a team.

Now, there are some practical ways of dealing with stress. Some years ago I had a man in my church who seemed to question everything I did. In fact, he questioned everything that anyone did. I found him to be very difficult; yet he was a good man. One day I asked him how his job was doing, and he told me the stress he had on the job and all the paper work he had. I asked him if he exercised at all, or had any physical activity. He told me he didn't. I suggested that he should do something. He took me seriously and took up racquetball. What a blessing! He found that it was just what the doctor ordered. He found himself being more supportive and less stressful. He kept everything in balance and realized how much more life was a blessing. Everyone around him found him easier to get along with, and he became a real blessing in the church.

> *"It's usually the little things that sometimes cause us the most stress."*

Here is a list of things you might look at, and some will be a blessing to you in dealing with stress. They seem simple, but it will help. It's usually the little things that sometimes cause us the most stress.

- ☐ Get up 20 minutes earlier.
- ☐ Wear good fitting clothes.
- ☐ Prepare your clothes the night before.
- ☐ Plan appointments ahead of time.

- ❑ Write things down.
- ❑ Avoid negative people.
- ❑ Learn to say no.
- ❑ Make meals simple.
- ❑ Ask for help with difficult jobs.
- ❑ Eliminate clutter.
- ❑ SMILE
- ❑ Have a sense of humor.
- ❑ Practice being friendly.
- ❑ Work on being optimistic.
- ❑ Feed some birds.
- ❑ Baby-sit.
- ❑ Tell a joke.
- ❑ Listen to someone's problems.
- ❑ Exercise.
- ❑ Clean your room.
- ❑ Go to a ball game and scream.
- ❑ Quit trying to perfect other people.
- ❑ Take a nap.
- ❑ Talk less and listen more.
- ❑ Compliment others on a job well done.
- ❑ Take a deep breath.
- ❑ Smell a flower.
- ❑ Take a walk.
- ❑ Read a good book.
- ❑ Set goals.
- ❑ Believe in yourself.
- ❑ Realize you don't have all the answers.
- ❑ Make duplicate keys.
- ❑ Make copies of important papers.

- ❑ Break large jobs into smaller ones.
- ❑ Look for the good.
- ❑ Speak a friendly word to someone.
- ❑ Teach a child to fly a kite or tie a shoe.
- ❑ Take time to play.
- ❑ Read a poem.
- ❑ Stop a bad habit.
- ❑ Strive for excellence, not perfection.
- ❑ Plant a tree.
- ❑ Stretch.
- ❑ Doodle.
- ❑ Know your limitations.
- ❑ Learn a new song.
- ❑ Cook a meal.
- ❑ Write to a friend.
- ❑ Take a bubble bath.
- ❑ Pet a friendly dog.
- ❑ Fix something that is broken.
- ❑ Listen to uplifting music.
- ❑ Order something new when eating out.
- ❑ Watch the sun set.
- ❑ Think ahead.
- ❑ Look at problems as challenges.
- ❑ Take a walk in the room.
- ❑ Bake a pie for a neighbor.
- ❑ Help someone change a tire.
- ❑ Look at the stars.
- ❑ Go on a picnic.
- ❑ Stop thinking tomorrow will be a better day.
- ❑ Read a Scripture.

- ❏ Play patty–cake with a toddler.
- ❏ Call someone to tell them you appreciate them.
- ❏ Put a rubber band on your wrist and snap it when you feel stress

Remember that stress is an attitude.

10

Where Ya' Lookin'?

In dealing with your attitude, you need to be focused. The Bible teaches you to look up, for your redemption is near. Now, that is spiritual. God doesn't expect you to be walking around with a stiff neck looking up into the sky, but it is a spiritual–mind set. Where you are focused is where you are headed. You need to look up and far enough ahead to see more than the situation you are in now. You need a general view to have direction and purpose for your life, and overcome these attitudes or behaviors that want to tear you from God's ultimate purpose for your life. Learn to look up.

When I first started driving and got my learner's permit, I needed someone to teach me to drive and be with me when I drove. We had a friend in the family who was a state trooper, and he volunteered to teach me to drive. He showed me all the safety things before starting the car, and a check list to have in my mind even before I turned the key. He shared some of the rules of driving and was very thorough in all his instructions. Now came the time I was allowed to take the wheel and drive. We were driving down a narrow road with one lane in each direction. It seemed so small. I never realized that until I was driving.

I had been on that road many times, but now I was driving. It never seemed this tight before, and I was a little nervous. It seemed like the cars coming in the opposite direction were so close. It was hard to drive too close to the right hand side of the road, as there was a ditch; and it seemed very deep. As I began to show some signs of being nervous, he told me to focus my attention further down the road. "Look up," he said, "quit looking at the ditch or the other cars, or the hood on your own car." He taught me to look up, further down the road, and to focus on that rather than the things immediately around me. He said that if I focused a little further down the road and looked up, I could be more aware of my direction, and with some experience I would be aware of all those things around me; but my focus needed to be down the road, looking in the direction I was going.

❑ **Look up, not down.** You know there are always people looking for the negative and not the positive. Remember, it is an attitude in looking up. Be an optimist, not a pessimist. Don't be a quitter. Stay in there and give it your best shot. It's just like driving that car; you need to look up. Looking down only focuses your attention on what is directly in front of you; and it may cause you to crash or worry about how quickly everything is going by. Be positive and have a positive attitude. Even when things look bad, be positive. You have heard about the optimist who fell off a twenty story building; and 10 floors down, someone heard him say that everything looked good so far.

One of my favorite stories I heard years ago was about two farmers that lived next door to one another. Andy was an optimist, and Daniel was a pessimist. Andy would wake up and see the sun shining and come out on the porch and throw his hands up and be thankful for the sunshine. Daniel would come out and see the sun and say that the sun would probably dry up the crops.

When it would rain, Andy would be thankful for the rain. Daniel would say that the rain would probably destroy the crops. This went on for thirty years. No matter what happened, Daniel would always find something wrong. Andy would say when things got bad, there was a light at the end of the tunnel. Daniel would say, that it was probably a train. For thirty years this went on and Andy was thinking that if he could do something so spectacular, that Daniel could do nothing but say something positive. So Andy came up with this great idea. Andy and Daniel always went duck hunting in the spring; and he was going to teach his dog a trick that Daniel would be so amazed he wouldn't be able to say anything negative. In fact, maybe it would leave him speechless. So Andy worked with his dog, Bullet, all winter. Every night he would pull down the shades and work with Ol' Bullet.

Finally the day came when the snow melted, and the first day of duck season arrived. There they all were in the boat: Andy, Daniel, and Bullet. Over head came a few ducks; and they shot their rifles and saw that they hit one, which fell about 25 feet from the boat. They were in about 12 feet of water at the time, and Andy got so excited. This was the moment he had been waiting for all winter. He said, "Bullet, go get him." The dog jumped out of the boat and tip-toed across the water, picked up the duck, and tip-toed back into the boat. Andy couldn't wait to see Daniel's face and hear what he had to say. At that moment Daniel turned to Andy and said, "He can't swim, can he?"

There are always some people who are always negative, and that needs to change. It is an attitude of mind. Learn to look up, and not down. Practice this in your life. Focus on where you are headed in life; and focus on the direction you are going. Learn to be positive and optimistic. Hang around with people who are positive, and let it rub off on you. Look for the bright side, and quit being so negative. Be a fighter, and tackle the challenges that life brings your way in a positive way. Stay in there when things get tough, and give it your best.

> *"There are always some people who are always negative, and that needs to change. It is an attitude of mind. Learn to look up, and not down. Practice this in your life."*

Two frogs fell into a deep cream bowl,
  One was an optimistic soul.
But the other one took the gloomy view,
  "I shall drown," he cried, "and so will you."
So with a last despairing cry,
  He closed his eyes and said, "Good-bye."
But the other frog, with a merry grin,
  Said, "I can't get out, but I won't give in!
I'll swim around till my strength is spent.
  For having tried, I'll die content."
Bravely he swam until it would seem,
  His struggles began to churn the cream.
On top of the butter at last he stopped,
  And out of the bowl he happily hopped.
What is the moral? It's easily found,
  If you can't get out—keep swimming around.

❑ **Look up, not around.** Those ditches and distractions are always there to take your focus off your direction and keep your spiritual eyes on the goal. As you learn to look up and not around, you see the great things that

God has for you and begin to deal with that anger, bitterness, and unforgiveness. It's not worth it. You often remain in anger, bitterness, or unforgiveness because you are focused on the things around you. You begin to fail because you get distracted.

The Apostle Peter gave you a good picture of this when he was in the boat with the other disciples. Jesus came walking on the water, and Peter asked if he could walk on the water also. Jesus said, "Come." Peter began to walk at the Word of the Lord. Then the wind began to blow, and the waves distracted him. He took his focus off the Lord and began to focus on the elements and those things around him. He began to sink, and the Lord helped him back in to the boat. There are things all around you to distract your focus. You will find yourself failing and sinking and allowing things like anger, bitterness, and unforgiveness to begin to drown you. It begins to take the life right out of you. Learn to look up and not around. Keep focused upon the Lord, and not all the distraction that life blows your way. There are many things that come against you every day. They come in forms of people, financial problems, relationships, jobs, and many other circumstances. They will always be there, just like the waves with Peter, or the ditches along the roads of life. Look up and not around. Know that God is in control of all things. All your worry will not help. Being angry, or bitter, will not help. Keep looking up in your attitude and manner of life.

❏ **Look up, not within.** It can be very discouraging to focus on yourself and all those things that you see within yourself that you know are there. God isn't finished with you yet. Reckon yourself dead. Keep focused up, and not within. The Holy Spirit is constantly leading you into all truth, and this is a process. Too many times you feel condemned by preachers because you do not come up to their standards. We all grow at different rates and in different seasons. Stop looking so close at yourself and at others. It becomes so easy for you to judge someone. Let the Spirit of God lead you and learn to pray for those who you see faults within. Looking up, and not within; keeps you focused in the direction of God; and He will take care of all those things within. They are there; don't deny it or think you are some horrible person. Keep focused.

❑ **Look up, not back.** Listen to the words of the apostle Paul in Philippians 3:13-14: *"Brethren, I count not myself to have apprehended: but this one thing I do, forgetting those things which are behind, and reaching forth unto those things which are before, I press toward the mark for the prize of the high calling of God in Christ Jesus."*

Paul was looking up and not back. He was keeping his affection and his focus upon the Lord. Everyone has some hurts and situations, or people who have done us wrong. In this life you will have trouble. Let your past be past at last. Every time the devil reminds you of your past, you remind him of his future. Learn from your past: all the hurts and even the victories. Learn from them and build upon them; but don't let them distract you from looking up, toward the goal. Keep focused. Refuse to dwell in the past. When you do, you bring back all those past emotions and feel them all over again.

Here is something very practical to help you. Don't go to sleep without praying and meditating upon the word. His mercy is new every day; but many times we take the past hurts to bed with us. The Lord tells us not to let the sun go down upon our wrath. That means that every day you need to keep focused. The past can be very hurtful and painful. It is your choice to either focus on that, or look up. It's all an attitude. It's your choice. God is there to help you, if you decide to focus upon Him. Even if you fail, He'll help you back in the boat. God is not there to condemn you if you fail. He wants to help you and love you if you, look up and not back.

Looking up means you are acknowledging God as your source. It's not always easy. It takes a lot of discipline and effort, because you get so weary. The pressure and the distractions are so strong at times that you just want to give in; but deep inside you want to succeed. Situations and people pull on your spirit, and you get so confused in the midst of it all. Those things may never change, but your attitude towards them can. The things that got through and made you angry will not affect you any more. The bitterness begins to disappear, because you're focused. Any unforgiveness is no longer a problem, and you freely forgive because you're headed in the right direction. It seems hard at first, but then you see the results and know they work. The principles really work, but you must learn them and practice them. These are things that demand discipline and time, but down the road you see your progress. This is not a formula for instant religion. You can be an overcomer or remain a victim. It's your choice. You can take the easy road and remain a spiritual cripple, or you can shake off the dust and get to work. It takes some courage and discipline, but the results are rewarding:

When things go wrong as they sometimes will,
When the road you're trudging seems all up hill,
When the funds are low and debts are high,
And you want to smile, but you have to sigh,
When care is pressing you down a bit,
Rest if you must, but don't you quit.
Life is queer with its twists and turns,
As everyone of us sometimes learns,
And many a failure turns about
When he might have won had he stuck it out;
Don't give up though the pace seems slow-
You may succeed with another blow.
Success is failure turned inside out-
The silver tint of the clouds of doubt,
And you never can tell just how close you are.
It may be near when it seems so far;
So stick to the fight when you're hardest hit-
It's when things seem worst
that you must not quit.

Accept life as a challenge. Stay in the fight and give it all you've got. Stick with the stuff. The only real loser in life is the one that quits. You can fail time and time again, but get back into the arena of life and ask God to help you one more time. God hasn't given up on you, so why should you? Keep your eyes on the goal and run the race. Others are depending on you. Look up, for the fields are ripe for harvest.

11

The Root

Anger, Bitterness, and Unforgiveness are all related. You may be dealing with one area, or possibly all three. They had to start somewhere. There was an event or circumstance that happened that you can possibly go back to and settle the matter. It could be that, over a process of time, one of these problems took hold in your life and needs to be faced and dealt with.

Because it is a root of bitterness, or anger, or unforgiveness, it will hinder many areas of your life. There are decisions you make everyday: big ones and little ones that are affected by a root or cancer in your life. It is imbedded into your spirit and, therefore, will affect all you do. *"The heart is deceitful, who can know it."*

When bitterness, or anger, or unforgiveness, is the root in a person's life, all he does is selfish and self-centered. The underlying motive in all he does or decide is based on self. He may try to hide his motive, but it is there. Some people try to turn everything around to make you look innocent, and how they were wounded; yet all the time they are not dealing with the real problem.

Some bitterness, or anger, or unforgiveness is so deep and hidden that others can feel they are at fault for years. If it gets to this level, you may need to take some time and really deal with this. You may have all the excuses in the world why you cannot afford to take the time, but you MUST. You'll pay for it, sooner or later.

Did you ever stop to think why you don't have a really close friend, or have people want to get close to you? The Bible teaches us that to have friends you must show yourself friendly. It also tells you not to make friends with an angry man. Pretty powerful, isn't it? Those roots of bitterness or anger also hinder your relationship with people.

Over the years I have dealt with all three of these areas. They must be faced head on and with complete honesty. The root must be dug out; and every time there is an opportunity for it to return, it must be dealt with immediately. If you make a mistake, you get back on track as soon as possible. Never let the sun go down without dealing with any area that can affect your spirit. Never let the enemy of your soul tell you that you cannot do it, or that you are a failure. If you must, agree with him quickly. Say

94

"Yes, I have failed but I'm still going to try harder". A righteous man falls seven times, but he gets back up again.

It is good to have a close friend who will be honest with you, someone who will help you deal in areas you struggle with, and not just someone who will agree with all your excuses. These areas are very serious and can ruin your whole life and keep you from your full potential in life. I have literally seen people drive themselves crazy, because they will not drop an offense. The mind is a very complex thing and will harbor things that should have been dealt with many years ago.

> *"It is good to have a close friend who will be honest with you, someone who will help you deal in areas you struggle with and not just someone that will agree with all your excuses."*

However, it is never too late, if you have a mind and a heart to repent. God says, "I'll restore all you have lost, and more." I have only touched the surface with this book. It will take the Holy Spirit to show you areas in your life. Throughout this book there might be areas you need to look into a little closer, or maybe to help someone else. Did you ever say, "What is wrong with my friend? Something must be eating at them." That's right, something might be eating away at their spirit. Be a friend and help them. If you truly have been a friend, you can go to them and ask the Lord how to handle the situation. Friendship, along with respect, must be earned. Ask yourself these questions when trying to help someone else in these sensitive areas:

❑ Is my heart right before God?

❑ Is my motive to help this person or to show him how spiritual I am?

❑ Have I earned the right to confront him in this area?

❑ Can I keep what he says in confidence?

❑ If he tells me there is no problem, can I just drop the subject and pray with him?

❑ Can I keep the relationship open with this person in case he needs me in the future?

You'll be surprised the people who need help in many of these areas. Possibly this book has helped you to see areas in your own life and has given you some keys to unlock some prison doors. The book may help you to save someone else's life. The principles work and will help you to care about people. God loves people. He may not like what they do at times, but He loves people.

May you go on to enjoy a full salvation and know the freedom God has for you and others. When Paul and Silas sang praises, every prison door was opened in the whole prison. May we be so totally free in God, that our desire is for every spiritual prison to be shaken and others loosed.

There was a little girl I heard about who had very bad eye sight. It was never noticed as the parents were poor and the problem went for quite some time undetected. At the age of six, when she went to school, the problem was discovered; and she was sent to the doctor for a pair of glasses. As she rode home in the car she couldn't help but be very excited. She saw things so clearly now. Things that were once a blur were now distinct. The whole world was now different: from looking at a book, to looking at the ocean, to looking into her mother's eyes. Everything was seen so differently.

May it also be with us as we view life. It's all there, but it's how we see it. We can miss out on a lot because we refuse to deal with the problem. God help us!

BIBLIOGRAPHY

Albert, R.E. & Emmons, M.L., *Your Perfect Right: A Guide to Assertive Behavior*.
> San Luld Ob. Spo: Impact, 1970.

Beall, James Lee. *How to Achieve Security, Confidence and Peace*.
> New Jersey: Logos International, 1978.

Bevere, John. *The Bait of Satan, Your Response Determines Your Future*.
> Florida: Creation House, 1994.

Cook, Jerry & Baldwin, Stanley. *Love, Acceptance and Forgiveness*.
> California: Regal Book, 1979.

Dean, Chuck. *Nam Vet, Making Peace With Your Past*.
> Oregon: Multnomah Press, 1990.

> *Funk and Wagnalls New Encyclopedia*, volume 24.
> Edited by Robert S. Phillips.
> s.v. "Star" and "Sun".

Halley, Henry, Dr. *Halley's Bible Handbook.*
Michigan: Zondervan Publishing House, 1965.

Hewett, James S., Gen. Ed. *Illustrations Unlimited.*
Illinois: Tyndale Publishers, Inc. 1988.

Hovey, Paul E. *The Treasury of Inspirational Anecdotes, Quotations, and Illustrations.*
Michigan: Fleming H. Revell, a division of Baker
Book House Co., 1987.

Matsakis, Aphrodite, Ph.D. *"Families on the Brink."*
American Legion Magazine, Sept. 1989.

Matsakis, A. PTSD: *A Complete Treatment Guide - Stress Management, Sleep Hygiene, Coping with Triggers.*
Harbinger Publications, 1994.

Tan, Paul Lee, ThD. *Encyclopedia of 7700 Illustrations: Signs of the Times.*
Illinois: RR. Donnelley and Sons, Inc. 1979.

The New Analytical Bible and Dictionary of the Bible.
London: John A. Dickinson Publishing Co., 1971.

The New Grolier Multimedia Encyclopedia, Release 6.
s.v. "Star" and "Sun".

Tribus, Paul A. *The Scars of War.*
Pennsylvania: Companion Press, 1991.

To order additional copies of

How to Overcome Anger, Bitterness and Unforgiveness

please send $8.95*
plus $2.00 shipping and handling to:

Paul Tribus
99 Sherwood Mall
Newport News, VA 23602

*Quantity Discounts Available

To order by phone,
have your credit card ready and call

1-800-917-BOOK